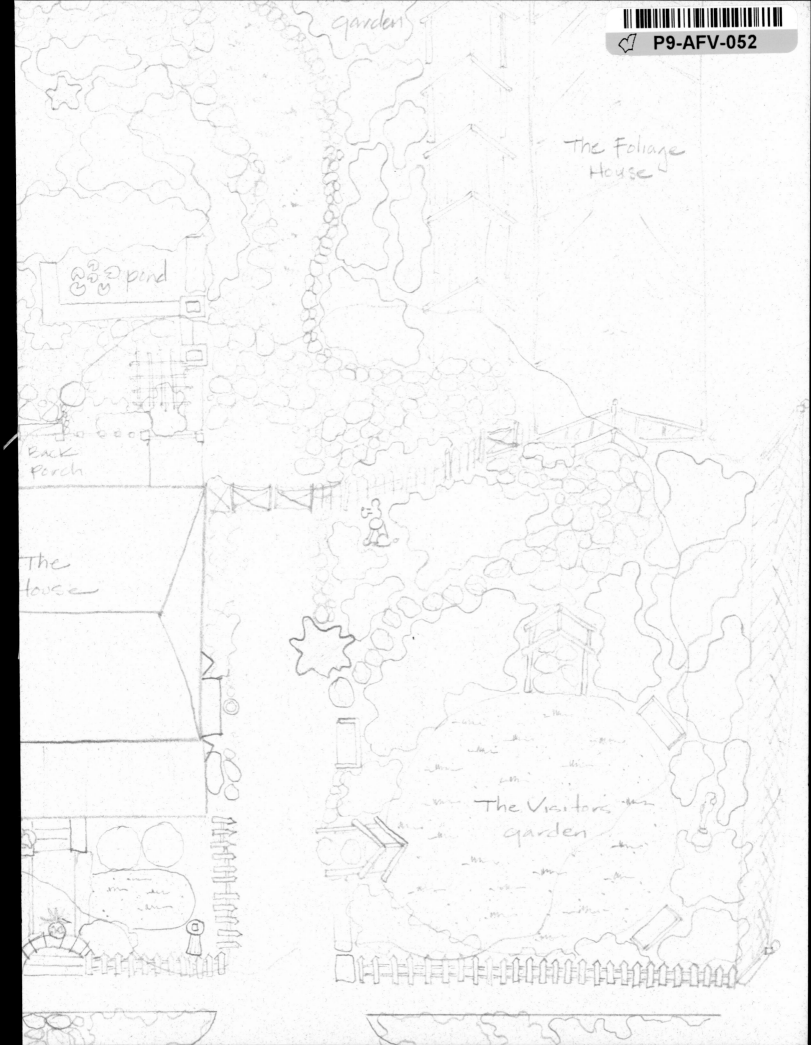

garden

The Foliage House

pond

Back Porch

The House

The Visitors garden

THE
WELL-PLACED
WEED

THE WELL-PLACED WEED

THE BOUNTIFUL GARDEN OF
RYAN GAINEY

PRINCIPAL PHOTOGRAPHY BY DAVID SCHILLING
DESIGN BY CHARLES L. ROSS

TAYLOR PUBLISHING COMPANY
DALLAS, TEXAS

"Path into the Visitors' Garden" appeared in *Perennials:
Towards Continuous Bloom*, copyright © 1991 Capability's
Books, Inc. Reprinted by permission of the author.

Published by Taylor Publishing Company
        1550 West Mockingbird Lane
        Dallas, Texas 75235

Designed by Charles L. Ross

Library of Congress Cataloging-in-Publication Data

Gainey, Ryan.
    The well-placed weed : the bountiful garden of ryan gainey / Ryan Gainey.
        p.   cm.
    ISBN 0-87833-837-3
    1. Gardens—Design.   2. Gardens—Design—Pictorial works.
    I. Title.
    SB473.G24   1993
    712'.6—dc20   93–10416
                                          CIP

Printed in the United States of America

10   9   8   7   6   5

this book
is dedicated
to my parents,
Ruth Catoe Gainey and Cecil Wilson Gainey,
their parents,
and my siblings,
who love the land as I do

Fulfillment 20

Appreciation 94

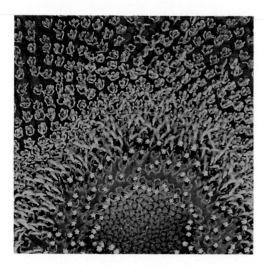

116 Reflection

146 Contentment

A
Personal
View
by Tom Woodham

In the summer of 1971, we were working on my father's farm to earn money for a trip to Europe and, at my mother's encouragement, Ryan Gainey participated in one of her favorite activities, the Lee County Flower Show. He swept the artistic awards and, with his avant-garde beard and dramatic flair, stirred up sleepy little Bishopville, South Carolina.

I've known Ryan for more than thirty years, through high school and college and several careers. His energy and creativity know no bounds, and he continues to stimulate people with his fresh approach to art and horticulture and life.

A side of him not generally known is his patronage of the arts in Atlanta on a very personal level. Over the past two decades he has commissioned countless pieces from artists who often needed the work. But that was secondary to the respect and admiration he held for the artist's skill in his or her medium. From Raku whistles of himself and each of his dogs to portraits, photographs, paintings, sculptures, whimsies, stage settings, poems, and illustrations, he has kept the spirit of art patronage alive.

With the zeal of a charismatic preacher, the insistency of a carnival barker and the energy of an erupting volcano, Ryan, with single-minded genius, lobs his creative salvos across the artistic sky as brilliantly as Helios drove his chariot and fiery steeds along the same trajectory. In the process he has shed light on countless subjects for numbers of people, while dressing up many festive occasions.

A natural salesman, Ryan lets his energy and enthusiasm generate a whirlwind of reasons why one's life would go sadly lacking if he or she did not have the special piece, philosophy, or experience in question. I remember, once, a lady telephoned our shop as soon as she arrived home. She was bewildered because she could not remember exactly why she had bought an item and wanted Ryan to tell her again why he thought she needed it.

A born organizer, he impatiently dives in and gets things going, later altering, refining, or completely redoing it according to his latest findings, learnings, and understandings. With Ryan, everything is passionate and whatever he is doing at the moment consumes him and everyone around him, dominating conversations as well as situations in a flurry of knowledge, inspiration, and original thought.

And so it is with gardening, his reigning passion. His wellspring of knowledge and imagination is forged into a personal philosophy in the fiery furnace of intense physical, mental, and spiritual work and determination. Not one to "light a candle and put it under a bushel," Ryan has learned that to do the most in the least amount of time he must spread his message to a larger audience. He eagerly shares his passion and his vision through a focused ability to make himself seen and heard. The world, not only of gardening but of life and beauty, is the beneficiary.

A
Plantsman's
Style
by Lisa Newsom

Style. Few words carry such a range of interpretations. It can describe a sense of fashion or the way we decorate our home. To me, though, it is the way we live—how we create our environment, how we push creative boundaries. The world of style delights most when it presents the rare individual who can spark trends and originate completely new looks. Ryan Gainey is such a person. His innate flair and fertile imagination have helped redefine the floral arts in the South.

Since founding *Veranda* in 1987 with Chuck Ross, I have been fortunate to have Ryan as supporter, friend, and important contributor. In fact, his artistry graced the premiere issue of the magazine—on the cover and in a ten-page spread entitled "Bridal Bouquets." Subsequent features of Ryan's designs included "Winter Interlude," "Floral Extravagance," "Bouquet de Soleil," "Exotic Dandies and White Wands," and "Summer Solstice," most of which were accompanied with lyrical prose by Ryan's former colleague and business partner, Tom Woodham.

I dare say Ryan's garden and designs have been featured more extensively than those of anyone else in his field. Regional, national, and international magazines and books often showcase his talent. Yet, with all his accomplishments and accolades, he remains generous with his time and creative ideas and continues to spread his inspired gardening message through lectures and demonstrations across the country.

Whether setting tables in a gift shop, installing elaborate gardens at the Atlanta Flower Show, designing a vignette for the High Museum of Art Antiques Show, or conceiving and producing the decor for countless charity balls, weddings, and parties, Ryan scrutinizes even the slightest of details with his expert eye. As his creativity unfolds, he seems perfectly at home and tranquil, belying the days of musing that have gone before.

I find it still more amazing to watch him work spontaneously. Whenever we photograph at his house, amid the cacophony of ringing phones, barking dogs, and climbing cats, I marvel at the finished product. His arrangements, interiors, borders, plates of food, or table settings evolve with apparent ease into studies of subtle complexity.

Once, on location for a photo shoot, a lady told me she had decoupaged a garden table using only pictures of Ryan's work clipped from the pages of *Veranda*. Now that's high praise indeed!

As an international plantsman, Ryan has been propelled into a social whirl, which he has embraced with aplomb. He dresses with flair—most often with a marvelously colored shawl, large-brim hat, and Armani sunglasses. A friend told me recently that she had observed him walking through the Paris airport and all eyes were on him. Another incident of superb style.

My favorite image of Ryan, however, is of him in his garden—working at a trot with all his dogs tagging along. I look forward to our occasional Sunday morning telephone chats to discuss a project or design. I only wish we could publish all the ideas that swirl endlessly in his head.

The beginning of gardening found its source in the story of Adam and Eve. In my garden, I recall the original paradise through garden gates and tiles.

There must be a single note that inspires a musician to write a piece of music, perhaps it is the singing of a bird, the sound of running water, the wind in the trees. Similarly, for each of us who make a garden, there must be that first seed that is planted. I remember my first efforts as a child: sprouting lima beans in a glass filled with cotton with the seed pressed against the glass. As the days passed, the seed swelled, cracked open, and the first tip of a root appeared growing down. Then came the first sight of green as the seed sprouted upward with its newborn leaves eventually reaching the light.

Many of us picked daffodils and took them to school where we stuck their stems into a bottle of ink to observe the absorption—the bright yellow daffodil became an iridescent green. We learned then our first lesson in color: yellow and blue make green. Nature, I found, had much to teach. My sixth-grade school teacher taught us how to identify trees by pinning the leaves we gathered onto construction paper and spray painting the paper with a fly sprayer. The perfect silhouettes we created became flash cards that challenged us to correctly identify which tree the leaf belonged to—a good lesson in association. But that was classroom work.

At home in the community where I grew up, there were many more lessons to be learned. We lived on the main road, turf then, later paved, and everyone else lived "back in the field," so called because at one time it was, indeed, a cotton field. In time far passed, it might have been a forest, later cultivated by man to produce a viable means to make a living. At some point, some farmer built a house, then there was another house, and eventually a community, which was named Lakeview. There was a lake on down the road, quite out of view, but a short walk provided a place for fresh water, fishing, and swimming. A church, a school, an established social order, all very functional and in keeping with what man has always done about creating order, and out of that order spurred creativity, observing the practical and, subsequently, seeking its beauty and creating a yard with flowers. I guess everyone had a yard, some were just prettier than others, better swept, more tended, loved. I cannot say exactly when it was, but I observed that beauty and the plants and asked, "What is that?" And there were three delightful country ladies in partic-

BEGINNINGS

ular who had very pretty yards bursting with flowers. They were their own gardeners—their lives were busy with raising children, cleaning house, cooking and growing vegetables, being quite dutiful about life—but these ladies took the precious time left over from each day to grow flowers.

Each one of them, Mrs. Faile, Mrs. Flowers, and Mrs. Floyd, had their own style based on the plants they loved to grow and each answered my question. They shared this love of gardening with me and taught me new lessons: How to root camellias under a mason jar beneath the eave of a barn. How to skillfully remove an African violet leaf from its crown and place it in an empty mayonnaise jar, a small amount of water in its bottom, tilted at a precarious angle in the window sill, covering the opening with foil. How to patiently wait while roots developed and the first new plantlets evolved.

"Can I have some of that?" "Well, yes. Come over and I'll show you how to separate a plant." And I went home with my first clump of thrift. Sure has been a long road to where I am now, yet how little has changed—the awareness of new beauty in a plant not known, the careful separation to divide and share, the sowing of cherished seed so that the memory stays intact, and, above all else, the patience required to appreciate the beauty that comes from growing and caring for what we each consider beautiful.

Neither of my grandmothers or my great-grandmothers probably knew too much about fancy things like aerial hedges, knots, or parterres, but they did know what they loved, and that was to grow flowers. My great-grandmama Johnson's garden was probably gathered from the woods and fields and a little swapping—to this day I long to be able to grow the phlox (*Phlox Drummondii*) that self-sowed all over her sandy-soil yard and provided a flower to wear to church in a coat lapel. How long ago and, though now I might wear a sweetheart rose in a silver vial on my coat, the fulfillment is the same. It reminds me of the poetic phrase now inscribed on my dining room wall, "The human heart is unknowable, but in my birthplace the flowers still smell the same as always."

Just now, the birds are singing, the ones that sing at dusk, and down the dirt driveway the most heavenly of scents fills the air. It was there this morning, or was it last night? Well it's back again.

"What is that?"—that scent—unnoticed until now, rising up out of the visitor's garden—devilwood (*Osmanthus americanus*)—smelling like honey long before the bees had gathered enough pollen to make their own. And just outside my kitchen window the bees are gathering sweet nectar from my Carolina silver bell (*Halesia carolina*) for their final trip home before the sun sets. "The flowers still smell the same as always."

I'm often asked when I began to garden, and I'm not quite sure. I can *remember*, as I just did, but I think it's better to ask, "where?" I can answer that question a lot easier because it is, then as now, from the heart.

So those were the "formative years" of blissful living and learning, then on to high school and the potential of college. After speaking with an astute guidance counselor, I found myself on the road to higher education at Clemson, where I studied ornamental horticulture. Then a four-year stint in the Navy landed me in Atlanta, where my true horticultural interest began to manifest itself.

Along with my friend, Tom Woodham, Eve Davis and I created and established Atlanta's standard of horticultural excellence, The Potted Plant, Ltd., still thriving as a source of eclectic delights, indoor foliage and flowering plants, and accessories for tasteful living.

Circa 1982, I moved from midtown into my first and only house in Decatur, where I took up residence in a two-story 1905 bungalow situated in the middle of three 50' x 150' city lots, with a beautiful white oak, a winged elm of good size, and a male American holly as my gardening companions. Formerly owned by the Holcombe family, the land was already endowed with horticultural merit—there were raised beds and glass hothouses for the production of cut flowers.

Not a bad way to begin creating a garden, and after the thoughtful advice of an early-on visitor, I have been careful to maintain the "history of the place" as I struggled to make my own garden. So here I am ten or so years later with a series of rooms, each with its own garden experience and each with a philosophy that aligns itself with the changing of the seasons and with each day and night that passes as the year evolves. I have traveled a great deal throughout the world, read numerous books, met other great gardening plantsmen and designers, 15

Gardens are the essence of change—as the seeds grow, the flowers bloom. It isn't like it was and neither will it be the same tomorrow, except in spirit.

and created a palette that allows me to paint in the best of medias—self-expression. Making a garden is indeed an art, and as much as that of the great gardeners, the works of painters and sculptors have been a valuable source of inspiration.

For me the visit I made to Claude Monet's garden at Giverny was the foremost catalyst. His garden opened my eyes to color. At first we choose our plants according to the color of flowers we like, but after that, the "painting" becomes so much more complex as one begins to embrace form, texture, shadows, stems, branches, light, wind, smell, bark. And once we combine the artistic eye and romantic soul with skillful horticultural manipulation and good gardening, each of us can make a garden.

However, all artists want to be asked to paint and create for other people, and I have been asked by many who have the great gift of appreciation. Those commissions have brought greater insight to the idea that is gardening, for I have worked in many geographical regions, both in America and in France. But wherever and for whomever, the reverence one must have for individual expression and a sense of place stays intact and allows me to create in the moment. I have learned, most importantly, to respect the land and work with indigenous plants and blend them with that which have been introduced, linking the garden to the architecture and style of house, and integrating the two ideas with personal taste to make a painterly setting that anyone would want to live in.

I guess that's why I also started The Connoisseur's Garden, which offers exciting plants (both new and old), appropriate garden appointments, and a design service. The true gratification, however, is the sharing that has evolved. And then there came The Cottage Garden, which brings all those flowers into focus on the table as a celebration of life. Whether it be a wedding, *un fete de Provençe,* or a thoughtful sentiment that can only be found in a garden-gathered nosegay, the bounty of the garden still continually overflows.

One must realize that the earth is the only planet that we know of in the universe that is covered with fertile soil. We have evolved, along with all other living things, to reach this high level of appreciation. And because we garden we have become the caretakers of the earth. With this awareness of our stewardship, we can perpetuate the idea of who made us. In the passing seasons, acknowledge each tree, each flower, each drop of water as they are transformed. Of all I have written in the book that I share with you, I can say this: "Only He can make a tree, but He also made the weed, and from those lowly weeds each of us can make our own garden and receive the bounty of the earth."

To the Gardener

There is a weed that
   grows
      along
        the
         g
          a
           r
            d
             e
              n
                path.

A passing thought of work
   well intended

in that crevice
   the joy of being
somehow left unintended.

And from that weed
   a flower is borne
and all our hopes
   are mended.

It brings to each of
   us
for all our plans
   well made
that such a lovely weed
   would somehow
      miss
        the
          s
           p
            a
             d
              e.

The pleasures sought
   from the garden
      wrought
   joy unending.

Cultivating this simple
   thought
      we become the
      weed
      well intended.

ryan gainey

Fulfillment

Fulfillment, or the idea of being satisfied, requires a great effort from those of us who create a garden. The creative process itself is the rarest form of fulfillment. All the hard work—preparing the soil, cultivating the thoughts, sowing the seed, gathering the flowers—has become for me a series of romantic experiences. Taking a long, luxuriant bath by candlelight at the end of the day, sponging away the work with the delicate petals of a peony blossom, imbibing its gentle soothing fragrance, puts me at heart's ease. Simultaneously, I realize that the time worth waiting for them to come into bloom is a lesson in the acquisition gardeners must always seek: patience. So one spends a moment indulging one's soul with gratification.

Much of the fulfillment that comes with gardening is visual, color being the primary and most obvious sensation. Color also gives us the truest form of self expression: one will often say, "I love that, it's *my* color." Our early gardening experiences are often growing plants from seed, thus we are able to easily grow the colors we love and express the joy we feel about ourselves. A simple sunflower in a pot, perhaps. We also learn the basic concept of cultivation—the act of making a garden. However, color takes on many hues and forms—more than the pure colors the child seeks—and we become aware of creating more complex gardens that weave in different plants. From that first catalytic moment until the present subtleties evolve. In that singular moment of ecstasy when we pluck the first flowers we grow, we recapture the childlike wonder within us all and step onto the path of continuous self-satisfaction.

In my own search for color, therefore, I have learned to appreciate the use of variegated plants, golden forms, the endless array of greens, grays, and blues. When fall comes, this rainbow moves back to the sky and the trees fulfill the dream that thoughts are made of. Time becomes itself as the season changes and we observe, absorb, and plant new thoughts. As I watch the leaves begin to fall I know that once again I will be able to see the patterns, the twigs, the branches, the bark, the silhouettes against a winter sky filled with gray.

I wonder, sometimes, what blue smells like. But when you close your eyes and take a whiff, waves of nostalgia take you to some other place in time, and the sensation that is color wanes as a thought-provoking aroma drifts up, enticing you into the past. I experience the titillation that the bee knows when he brings himself to the flower and says let's make a seed. So can the wind, with the slightest of breezes, refresh a memory that is the afterthought of a hard day's work.

I have grown and cultivated my garden with all these ideas—memory, textures, sensory experiences—intact. I have learned how pleasant it is to nurture the nuances that each flower can give—its color, its fragrance, its being.

The seasons change, bringing new scents, from "the sweet breath of spring" to "wintersweet," completing a year in the garden's life. With that, one learns to embrace bare branches, bark, seed, the color of the seeds themselves, flowers, plants going to seed, knowing the buds and watching them swell into fulfillment. I wait with anticipation for the flowering of the datura and the vespertine essence of its fragrance, and the four-o'clocks that tell the time of day. I always remember to plant the moon vine seed: One can imagine the moment that inevitably comes when out into the garden you go to pick their purest white, enticingly delightful blossoms to bring to the table, blossoms that will pass away and fade back into the moonlight.

Gardening in window boxes is a charming aspect of cottage gardens that allows for seasonal changes and thus keeps the garden in bloom almost all year.

Path into The Visitors' Garden

Begonia grandis in bloom in September.

How long did it take God
to create the earth
and find a way to let humanity
make a path on which to walk?

How many words would it take
to write about my garden
in its totality?
Words would be like leaves,
all might fall from the trees
before
I had time
to fully express my thoughts.
The truth is,
there are no words—
for so many aspects of the garden are
new,
gradually being
filled with their own truths.

24

My garden efforts
are just now in their eighth year;
they began
with the creation
of my first garden room.
Now
the total garden picture has
evolved
into
a series of rooms,
each with its own
horticultural qualities,
architectural elements,
and garden accessories.
All
filled with delight—
a series of captured thoughts and
sought-after dreams.

The Visitors' Garden,
about which I write,
is intended to be
a quiet place.
In a verdant surround
and slightly enclosed,

it is
visible from the sidewalk
of a quiet street.
This small enclave
invites you
to come in
and visit
without intruding.

Nostalgia
has already found
its place
here
for I can easily remember
so many lovely settings
and permeating scents.
Two dear friends were wed here,
when there was only a row of
standard tree roses on the street;
the roses are gone
now,
but that memory
is a part of the garden
only time can cultivate
in our hearts.

Opposite: Magnolia tripetala is one of the many trees that grows in the visitors' garden.

The native plant *Aesculus parviflora* in spring.

Gordonia Lasianthus, another native, blooming in August.

The esoteric qualities
of Nature
have become a living dream
filled with subtleties
that only She
can
provide, a lesson
so long in the learning,
a vision just now being seen.
When I look
into this setting,
I see the realization
of nature and humanity
becoming
one.

28

Hydrangea arborescens 'Annabelle' in midsummer.

Here the colors in spring are
a blending of
greens,
gray-greens,
chartreuses,
golds,
russets,
browns,
and ambers.
Soft sunny colors,
both cool and warm
(like the memories
time cultivates).
Even the rains are
like a drizzle of dew
that
falls
from heaven.
I have taken
my palette from the colors that
come from nature
Herself.

We
cannot be taught
but we can be
instilled
with the pleasures of learning
and therefore
seeing.

29

Even in the hottest summer
these same soothing colors
give us the essence
of spring,
but without so many flowers.
In the fall,
the leaves drained
of their green
dreams cover the ground
with the same color scheme;
one walks
on a carpet
made for a king.

In winter,
bare branches,
exfoliated trunks,
inner structure,
and seeds
decorate
the garden with subtlety,
and suddenly
on a warm winter day
a fragrance comes
from a flower just then
seen. The light
changes through every season
and we must find another way of
seeing.
Vision and ideas
have become
an everlasting reality.

I have not named
the trees,
or leaves,
or flowers.
The bulbs
are not called by name.
Nothing has been said
of the effort
or all the labor therein.
I have given
and I have taken
and I have received
a dream.

Left: Edgeworthia papyrifera with
newly opening buds in March.

Perspectives

are a valuable visual aspect in a garden. When I added a series of peaked structures down the path of the dry wall garden, I wanted this series of six rustic arbors to be the same height. With a subtle slope in the land and an eye to keep them all level, I discovered a forced perspective, with all six visible simultaneously. So now I have a subtle, lengthened view of the walk and the illusion of a deeper sense of space. A delight in itself and an opportunity for more vines as well, making the garden richer architecturally and horticulturally.

Japanese rose, *Kerria japonica* 'Plentiflora,' in bloom in early spring at the entrance to the arbors.

The dry wall garden is planted with a variety of flowering shrubs for different seasons, many of which are fragrant. Plume poppy (*Macleaya cordata*) rambles among them, keeping the planting loose and airy as the wind moves through their silver-backed leaves, capturing light and movement. In August, a planting of *Lycoris squamigera* provides a sense of magic as the three-foot lilies add an unexpected delight.

*G*rowing, flowering shrubs for seasonal interest make for a versatile garden, and this nice, pale pink form of *Weigela florida* is a superb addition for any plantsman who wants to have "old-fashioned" plants as a part of a picturesque setting. When cutting three- and four-foot flowering branches for the house, I am simultaneously pruning the plant to keep it in form, combining the ideas of good gardening and the gifts that it offers.

Opposite: Along the path opposite the dry wall, a mixed planting of *Viola* 'Prince John,' *Aquilegia canadensis,* and *Tulipa* 'Fireflame' provide an exciting color combination.

An old, "found" arch of iron and wire provides a support for *Rosa* 'New Dawn' with *Rosa* 'Ballerina' growing amidst a wooden chair that was here when I moved in.

ative shrubs are often the best choices for making a good garden, and, for me, *Hydrangea quercifolia*, or oak-leaf hydrangea, is a favorite. It blooms in May and provides strong texture in the summer, beautiful fall color, and interesting exfoliating bark for the winter—four good reasons to grow this delightful shrub.

Most garden shrubs bloom on the past season's growth: flower buds for the next season are produced during the summer growing season. Any pruning should be done when the shrub is in flower, whether you cut one-foot stems or long branches. Again, it is a way to keep your plant in form and to reap its bounty—its flowers. The idea is to allow plenty of time after blooming to grow and produce an abundance of flowers for the next season. Always remember that the earlier a shrub blooms, the new growth that follows will be making those buds, so "a cut in time gives nine," for if you wait too late you will be cutting off your flowers that will come next season.

Right: One of my favorite one-time bloomers is *Rosa* 'May Queen,' rambling over the original greenhouse, a dug-out built around 1919, with *Hesperis matronalis*, or dame's rocket, blooming in the foreground.

Borders

Borders or herbaceous flower beds, are better experienced on a trip where the season is shorter and perhaps cooler than in what we endure in the Southeast. After the struggle ended to work within that concept, I have found delight with mixed borders of flowering shrubs, self-sowing annuals, and some choice herbaceous plants. Over a six-year tenure, a great deal of pleasure and satisfaction comes from making good choices of plants that offer a variety of effects. Here, foliage provides as many effects as flowers. Clipped evergreens, tutors for vines, and arbors for roses give architectural substance to the borders. Being cognizant of durable and later blooming plants, I have extended the growing season well into September. This winter a few relocations were made to eliminate non-obvious mistakes. The *Hydrangea aspera villosa*, suffering from too little sun in the visitors' garden, will be quite happy here, and two very good, multitrunk *Lagerstroemia* 'Meyer's Hardy Lavender' were planted on either side of the arbor where *Rosa* 'Gloire de Dijon' grows vigorously, as pictured below.

Top: Before. *Opposite:* The borders in late July reflect the infusion of foliage and forms. Bright pink *Phlox paniculata* blooms profusely for four to six weeks (*right*) and *Hibiscus syriacus,* a double pink form of althaea, flowers equally as long (*left*).

*P*atterns are as integral to the design of a garden as the formation of a leaf or flower. Whether those patterns are formally shaped or amorphous, the design on a garden pot, or the shape of stones laid in a path, a garden cannot hold itself together without them. The circular pattern in the center of the borders is reinforced by cast iron edging stones with a scallop shape—another pattern. Even the tulips mimic this idea, but the rigidity is broken by the spilling growth habit of the violas. The radiating cast stone slabs expand this circular pattern even more, with the lead-in and -out using the same slabs to create a simple straight-line walk through this garden setting.

This Portuguese jardinière has been a focal point at the cross axis of the borders since they were made. Different plantings are implemented for seasonal change. Both these pictures show violas, pansies, and tulips with a self-sowing *Euphorbia epithymoides* given by a gardening friend.

Spiraea × Bumalda 'Gold
Flame,' *Dianthus barbatus*
'Newport Pink,' hybrid iris,
cool-weather annuals and roses
are a part of the spring palette
in the borders.

*D*eveloping a garden from past memories and present travels brings both a sense of nostalgia and new ideas to its making. Gathered seed from a trip or an afternoon walk or ordered from a catalogue provide me the opportunity to keep treasured thoughts intact and satiates the desire we all have to "grow our own from seed."

Gathered and saved, seed enables me now to have my own special poppies, sunflowers, cleomes, and cornflowers. So each year we sow seed, send a few out, and manage to add one or two new plants. I like having a seed box too, so that on winter days I can contemplate when and where the seeds will be planted and then take delight in the memory of when I first saw them in bloom.

Above: This *Digitalis* × 'Emerson White' grew here when I came and is now a good companion to *Silybum Marianum* from Barnsley House. *Right:* Equally happy together is the *Spiraea* × 'Limelight' in between fennel and this self-sown euphorbia (*left*).

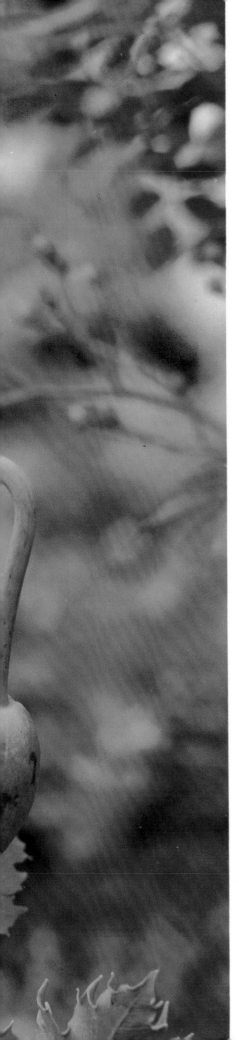

Poppies are easily grown as a cool-weather annual by blowing the seed from the palm of you hand wherever you want them to grow. At left is a double red, peony-flowered form collected from Monet's garden at Giverny. Nasturtium (*below*) can be started early indoors and planted out after frost or seeded directly in. I like this bright yellow 'Whirlybird' in the border, but in other parts of the garden we grow 'Empress of the India,' 'Alaska,' and a pale yellow one that is worth searching the seed catalogues for.

*E*very plant one admires cannot be bought, sometimes it is "found," perhaps in a deserted garden or by someone else who is willing to share. Railroad tracks, ditch banks, and woodland walks are sources of discovery. The plants I find in forgotten or untouched places are as important to me as when they were seen and written about by early plantsmen. Who knows what the Native Americans called wild plants, but such names and the old uses for them make for story telling and folklore. This chrysanthemum on the left is such a storied plant to me—found in Mrs. Gatlin's yard, where I realized

its potential as a good garden plant. It blooms in July with white shasta-daisy-like flowers, tolerates full sun and drought, produces adventitious plantlets at most terminals and provides an evergreen matte in the winter garden. Is there anything else you might desire? Well, the story is, Mother Gatlin shopped through the market bulletin, spied a daisy ad and set out to see. It was $4.00 a pot (worth $40 then), an appalling price. Thank goodness she spent the money because now we have what is called *Chrysanthemum maximum* 'Ryan's White.' Yet to make the story more historical, perhaps we should call it "Miz Gatlin's Daisy." This iris is the prettiest blue

Iris siberica I've seen of all those selected to date. It was found by one Bob Hill and given to Goodness Grows, who shared a piece with me, so now I divide it and increase the numbers of clumps I have. If you catch me on a good day I might share it.

The hollyhocks with a kiss of peach are from seed "taken" from a plant in Rachel Jackson's garden at The Hermitage and are thought to be original to the place. Historically she would have grown these old-fashioned singles—even if they aren't the exact seed, it makes for a good story about found plants and the gardening heritage they may bring.

ontinuous change is as much the motif in a garden as a recognizable tune taken from a musical score. Having gardened for a decade now, I've learned to accept these changes for their "plant" value. Learning how plants grow, spread, tolerate, and, sometimes, give completely up on me, I am now the dutiful pupil. Sure, mistakes have been made, but if I find understanding about what each plant needs, I'll probably get a lovely bouquet of flowers. Do not be afraid to try, and before you experience failure, observe! Move things around to where they should be—this is an aesthetic as well as a horticultural endeavor.

Prune diligently and carefully, and if you cut too soon or too late you'll have to learn the lesson. Reading good books makes good sense, but read in order to understand. Look at pictures and visit gardens, but look beyond the pretty and, again, observe to understand. Put in, take out, change, relocate, recombine—and constantly refine.

Phlox paniculata (*background and right*), common purple, and *Rudbeckia* 'Goldsturm' (black-eyed Susan) are summer staples in the borders and continue to bloom when *Hydrangea paniculata* 'Grandiflora,' trained as a standard, blooms gloriously white in early August.

56

Opposite: Rosa 'Nastrama,' dame's rocket, and peony 'Felix Crouse' blooming in May about the antique garden bench and rough-hewn arbor.

*L*ife in a garden would not be complete without its birds, bees, and fireflies—and, for me, a menagerie of dogs and cats. They're all well fed and seem not to bother each other, but the exceptional chase keeps everyone on their toes. Many gardeners place emphasis on plants to attract particular insects and other garden visitors, which is a fine idea. I seem to have an adequate number of fireflies, bees, and other such, but there's that cabbage moth that makes the hair on the back of my neck rise up. Well, a few years ago I was given a new plant, apparently a vine. After a couple of years it came into bloom, and one afternoon I saw several cabbage moths seemingly attached to the flowers. It seems the inside of the bloom of this vine has a trap: as the moth searches for the sweet essential nectar, its proboscis gets caught—the moth's final hours are wasted in attempted escape. What's wrong with growing a plant as a natural predator to keep those "cute little butterflies" at bay? Guess what its common name is? Cruel vine. Botanically it's called *Arauja sericifera* and makes beautiful and quite interestingly shaped seed pods in the fall.
Such are the pleasures of gardening.

Top: Cruel vine. *Above:* Willie constantly relocates himself to take advantage of the warm sun as he views the arbor that leads to the oval and the bird feeder. (He wouldn't scratch a flea.)

Rosa 'Gloire de Dijon' blooms profusely in June, but its great beauty is its copper foliage that comes in April and recurs throughout the gardening season. The cone-shaped topiaries are formed from variegated euonymous, which were ultimately unsuccessful as clipped forms and were given away.

The Oval

garden is directly adjacent to the borders and is the site of a past greenhouse. Like many of my early garden ventures, it seemed another site for more flowers—and a new pattern. Using what is at hand is a good idea—a form of recycling—so two-inch clay pots from the growing days were in abundance and became the edging. Now there's a rather smart mowing edge of stone but the pots remain—sort of a whimsical touch. First-year flowers, next-year grass, alas, some breathing room, and a place to lie down, look at the sky and frolic with Rosemary, Hollyhock, Snapper, and Joe-Pye. Sounds like I fell into a flower bed by mistake, but they're the resident menagerie and path finders (path makers might be more accurate).

This garden was the last to come into form, and by this time I had discovered a little restraint and understanding of how to use golden foliage plants. So this garden has an astute horticultural focus, as the shrubs are chosen for white flowers and golden foliage. There's also some very definite "bedding in" for spring and fall. I created this term to describe a planting style that would give a flower bed the romantic nuance of a mingled mass and spilling over. My friend Rosemary Verey would say, "good bedfellows, I think."

The oval in its first year with a pair of antique terra cotta urns filled with margarite daisy, lobelias, *Helichrysum*, and geraniums. The poppy is *Papaver Rhoeas*—the Flanders field poppy—which still reseeds in this garden.

63

*H*ydrangea *arborescens* is among my favorite garden shrubs. As a native species it's prolific and happy in the visitors' garden. Below is the cultivar 'Annabelle' at the entrance to the new garden where the herbs were originally. This hydrangea is one of many shrubs and trees that blooms on the current season's growth. So any time before they break dormancy and slightly afterwards they can be pruned to the desired height or form without destroying the flower buds for that blooming season. It's rather nice that some plants have managed to escape our best intentions. However, if you get clipping happy in June, stay away from 'Annabelle,' vitex, crepe myrtle, the peegee hydrangea, and others that fall into this garden group.

Right: This pattern of golden barberry (*Berberis aurea*) can be viewed from the street through the *claire-voie* in the cherry laurel hedge.

*S*pring is certainly the most fulfilling time in the garden and the oval does have a glorious moment with pink and white sweet williams bedded in with "sown-*in-situ*," purple-frilled poppies (*Papaver somniferum*), but October reflects the fall sky and the intense purple and yellows one comes to expect in the South. What a color scheme: the golden and variegated plants against clipped hedge walls of cypress and laurel.

A view from the street through the *claire-voie*—a delightful discovery for passersby on the street walking past the cherry laurel hedge. This peep through provides a long axis through the oval and the vegetable garden entrance made of native cedar (*Juniperus virginiana*).

Fall in the oval, with golden *Chamaecyparis* 'Crippsii', fastigiate American box, and white *Eupatorium rugosum* bedded in with *Cleome* 'Violet Queen', gomphrena, stone mountain daisy (*Viguiera porterii*), and Mexican bush sage (*Salvia leucantha*). The cleome and Mexican bush sage, and other tall, informal, relaxed plants, make an interesting foil against the strong, defining hedge.

A corridor behind the borders serves as a cross axis through the garden, with the hedge of the borders on one side and the vegetable garden wall and my greenhouse walls on the other. Two narrow beds are filled with herbaceous geraniums, *Phlox divaricata,* and *Dianthus* 'Bath's Pink.' The trelliage facade of the greenhouse is now covered with passion vine, *Vitis vinifera* 'Purpurea,' various purple-flowered clematis, and *Rosa* 'Mermaid.' The Italian wall pot exudes *Euphorbia Cyparissias* and restrains its aggressive garden habit. On its down side, there are fulfilling views of the borders, the oval, and the vegetable garden, and uphill, simple picket gates take you into the terrace or backyard garden, providing an escape from the complexities of garden life where one can sit under a grape arbor and dream of Provence.

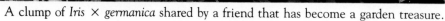

70 A clump of *Iris × germanica* shared by a friend that has become a garden treasure.

The Vegetable Garden

with its box parterre was inspired by the potager at Barnsley House, which in turn was inspired by the plantings of vegetables at Villandry. Not unlike the other rooms in my garden, there have been many changes over the years. What I grow now fills my present needs, to simply have enough vegetables and herbs to satisfy the table as the season changes. There are fewer types of lettuce, but more of the varieties that work better for me. One season for leeks and onions was enough, because peas were easier and more bountiful in the space. The rustic trelliage is now consumed with a selection of climbing roses like 'Cécile Brünner,' 'Fortune's Double Yellow' and 'Silver Moon.' The *Clematis texensis* 'Duchess of Albany' covers a fair amount of space and mingles happily with the cypress vine that blooms in late summer. The entrance arbor is becoming overgrown with climbing fern and potato vine (*Solanum jasminoides* 'alba'). The diamond box patterns that once housed black-seeded Simpson lettuce now spill over with violas and Shirley poppies in spring, *Zinnia peruviana* from Monticello in the summer, and, in August, *Lycoris aurea* rising up out of nowhere to delight the eye. It's February and the peas are in (I hope not too soon). Seeds are ordered for the annual spring plantings and soon I must divide my three remaining yellow-berried Frais de Bois, for I would never want to be without their delectable flavor in late May.

Above: The vegetable garden in its infancy. *Right:* The old stick trelliage gradually went and this native juniper took its place.

72

Viola tricolor and black-seeded Simpson lettuce grow happily together beneath the standard rose 'The Fairy' in the diamond box parterre.

Petite pois and sugar snaps provide several eatings for spring dinners, but may get eaten while I'm picking.

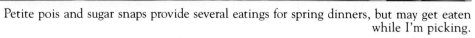

76

A very vigorous 'Brown Turkey' fig grows in the barn garden, a layered slip from Smith's daddy. There's nothing like fresh figs. On a trip to California I observed this variegated form called 'Panache.' Isn't it wonderful! So now I have three.

Gourds were grown one year on the trellises but proved to be too rambunctious. A few were dried and hand-painted for fun.

Oak leaf lettuce and Frais de Bois are one of several combinations that are planted in the spring.

Overleaf: I plant heirloom tomatoes—Yellow Pear, White Beauty, and Ox-heart—on the trellis after the peas are gone. *Salvia Vanhouteii* is a superb late bloomer and good container plant to move about and fill an empty spot.

81

A Wedding

party in the garden and from the garden is one of the finest forms of fulfillment. Over the years I've helped bring to fruition that moment of marriage and celebration and flowers from my garden. Getting there means several stops, picking sweet peas and thistles from the side of the road, finally spotting a pure white one for the bride's bouquet. Off the expressway and down a country road and right in front of you is a field of Queen Anne's lace. Not going too much "store bought" about this one. One more turn and look at that wonderful stone tobacco barn at the entrance to the farm. We should make a "gathered" bouquet and hang it on the door. So we did and immediately set the ambience for this time of celebration. Coming up to the house the side garden was filled with buckets and buckets of garden-grown roses, and tubs of ivy and hydrangea all gathered by friends as a gift from their own gardens. How enriched the whole experience was by such bounty and love shared.

A "gathered" bouquet of common perennial pea (*Lathyrus latifolius*), the annual *Ami majus*, and oak-leaf hydrangea.

*H*aving wonderful settings to work with is artfully stimulating and so my approach was to create a series of *tableau vivants* in the house. The Chinese porcelain bowl in the entrance hall seemed to be waiting for the peonies. The landscape painting in the living room was a perfect background for the combination of rhododendron, *Nicotiana langsdorfii,* and the seed pods of money plant. The dining room, with its collection of botanicals, allowed for a slightly wild melange of grasses, *Allium,* and red hot poker.

$\mathscr{R}$olling hills and a charming vegetable garden created the landscape setting for a delightful lunch following the wedding. Rosemary rings and wreaths with feverfew were made for the children in the party with a mixture of roses, sweet peas, and lady's mantle for the maid of honor. For the bride, a hand-carried bouquet of garden-grown calla lilies, hosta leaves, and 'New Dawn' roses picked from the garden wall. All thoughtfully gathered together and bound with french ribbons and a few lover's knots.

L ovingly decorated with more 'New Dawn' roses and the rose 'Ballerina,' the cake itself seemed to have grown from the garden just for this moment. It was as if all the forces of magic came together in a state of bliss that later seemed to be a dream. In reality it's why we all should have a garden and celebrate life.

Appreciation

Growing up wasn't so bad after all. Yes, it was a lot of work, sometimes hard work, but the labor was shared among all of us. Daddy plowed the rows with a borrowed mule (I'm sure in exchange for some of the crop) and one of us dug the hole, another dropped in the correct amount of seed per hill, yet another filled the hole, and then we all weeded. Nothing like planting time. Often we would go to Aunt Marie's and help there. My most vivid memory of that time was turning the sweet potato vines in the early morning, staying well abreast of Sue, the mule. At the end of the summer we heeled in those potatoes along with the last of the tomatoes, picked green, before the frost fell on them.

Sitting on the back porch shelling those peas was a time for talking and listening to the radio, seeing who could shell the most, the quickest. More than once we took a chance on getting done early by burying some unshelled beans beneath the hulls. Never did get away with it, all the while learning the virtues of being honest. Every summer we planted okra, squash, corn, cucumbers, melons, beans, and tomatoes. I didn't like okra then, but now I love it, having learned to appreciate its distinct taste—but that's a part of growing up. Now I know a lot more vegetables and my taste buds now incorporate condiments beyond salt and pepper, but they remain the basic ingredients for just good food.

The coming together at the table for a freshly picked meal of corn, rice, beans, and fried chicken was a time of thankfulness. More than just a meal, it was being together at the kitchen table sharing the bounty of the garden. Having a flower garden was as viable to me then as it is now, but there were always a few allotted spots for flower beds. Canna lilies always grew outside the back porch and were kept well watered, as that was a convenient place to pour the water that might have sat in the bucket all day and had gotten too warm to drink. You see, there was always fresh water from an artesian pump shared with our neighbor. We had water, pumped by hand, for drinking, cooking, bathing, and for the washing of clothes.

A lot has changed since then, but I still grow canna lilies to keep the memory intact. The tomatoes I grow now are heirloom types, though they never taste as good now as then. Growing a garden from seed as I do now with vegetables perpetuates my agrarian roots, and though gardening for me now feeds the eye and the soul, the pleasure from the hard work and its bounty was planted in my heart long ago. So my vegetable garden has evolved beyond simple rows into a room enclosed by brick walls and trellises and a series of patterns made of box hedging and stone edging. Skillfully clipped diamonds with topiaried standards of roses, underplanted with chartreuse lettuce and nasturtiums, make for a more artful form of vegetable gardening. The petite pois trellises are now the frames for tomatoes to scramble up and get the summer sun they need to ripen into bright red morsels of edible flesh with fresh basil aplenty. It's still just as much work as it was in the past, because making a vegetable garden is working with annuals, both for spring and summer. A constant replanting to bring the garden to the table. There's nothing quite like homegrown. No, I don't grow my own corn or okra, but there're thymes, rosemary, and mints all thoughtfully intermingled with summer annuals that bring the simple flowers of species zinnias, marigolds, and sunflowers.

In a way, I guess it doesn't matter what you grow, but, indeed, that you take the time to plant the seed. Watching it grow, you never lose the childlike wonder that is a part of each of us. Sometimes when I'm out there in the heat, I can't help but wonder how we worked so much to "bring in the sheaves," but in that moment comes the contentment of knowing that the work must go on in order to receive. Times have changed, they say. Things are not what they used to be. Not true, I say, because one must take the time to plant a seed, watch it grow and flower, consume the hour—and if you think it's merely a weed don't pull it too soon. It could be just out of place.

Sunflower Legend

My own garden is a small and private (secular) place. When I am awakened each day by the crescendo of singing birds and rays of early morning light, I am indeed in my own world. Yet I still experience the whole—knowing that the garden only has arbitrary boundaries around it and remains vitally in nature—and I try to learn all I can about how to preserve this earthly paradise, its lands, waters, forests, and sky. Each of us must do our part, but the responsibility we take on must be endogenous and perpetual. Sometimes a story will enlighten me and make me more astute about my place and part of this earth. Understanding may come through simple storytelling, like a nursery rhyme or fable. Mythology is one of the earliest forms of explaining who we are and what our relationship is to Mother Earth. We all know the story of Demeter and her beloved daughter Persephone, whose abduction by Hades and subsequent release brought about the change of seasons.

But one of my favorite stories from folklore is the Native American legend of the sunflower. The flower came to the earth from the sky, brought as seed and planted by the Great Creator to help Mother Sun dry up the earth. The earth had been devastated by the rains that almost covered Man and all living things when the Great Creator became unhappy with Man for his unwise ways.

The little seed resembled the Sun and became tall to reach the Sun—her friend. The new flower also became a friend to Man, who was able to use her leaves, seeds, flowers, and roots to live. She was named "sunflower." And every day, the sunflower would lift her head towards the Sun to follow her friend's path.

This legend is about our elemental connections to nature—the way a seed becomes a flower is transmuted into a meaningful tale, a myth, often retold. Through our interaction with nature—even the simple act of thumbing a seed into the soil—we help to keep the earth alive and we share its pleasures. Whether through tales or actions, we must remember what a wonderful place the earth is and that we are her keepers.

Our own self-branching, tall-growing sunflowers found in a defunct garden.

Sunflowers

mirror the summer sun that fills those long hot days with golden light. Like the Native American legend, as a form of storytelling I, too, have woven this flower of summer into the celebration of my own garden.

Every summer I grow my own collected seed and plant them in sunny locations throughout the garden. I've been traduced into growing selected forms that are now available in catalogues, as I wanted to have all types that were available. One summer I decided not to grow them at all and it was as if the sun never shined. Now I can live with all those selected forms but not without the sunflower itself, although it's now represented by just two types, one remembered, the other found. The latter was on a trip into the Georgia countryside when I spied this golden sunflower tree about seven to nine feet tall, self branches with dozens of small flowers smothering the mother stalk. People inquire, and, once I have diligently sown the seed, as the birds love this one as much as I, the remaining seeds are mailed out to others who wish to have them.

About four years ago, I was recalling the sunflower that I knew as a child. Well, I don't go home as much anymore, but I called my sixth-grade school teacher. She was the only person I knew who would know what I was talking about. Sure enough, she did, and thought she remembered a spot where she had seen them growing along the side of the road. However, she said that it may not be possible because the Department of Highways mowed so much that they might have cut them down. At any rate she spied a patch, watched them carefully, and one day in the mail some seed heads came. So now I have them both: small-growing and self-branching with tall-growing and self-branching—lifting their heads to the sky to celebrate the summer sun.

Helianthus sp., *Rudbeckia* 'Goldsturm' and *Zinnia linearis* create a kaleidoscopic pattern floating in a hand-thrown bowl.

100 Pesto from the garden is a gift of the summer sun in a sunflower basket filled with seeds for birds. The stalk is simply curled over to meet the head.

Sautéed sunflower buds (*top*) are considered the most potent of aphrodisiacs. Scooter, like most cats, feels at home on the table, wondering when dinner will finally be served.

102

The sunflower is artistically interwoven into several vignettes in the garden, including a *paràsoleil*, a place to sit, a water vessel, and depictions in terra cotta and concrete. Some are garden-functional; others are just to please the garden. *Far right, top:* The fiery red nasturtium is 'Alaska,' a variegated form. *Far right:* The concrete sunflower is partially obscured by *Rosa* 'Madame Pierre Oger,' *Digitalis purpurea,* and *Euphorbia cypressifolia.*

Supper for the Summer Solstice

The sun is with us every day, all year round, sometimes masked by clouds and rainy days. We don't see it, but yet there is light. In the summer more than any other time, it stays with us longer to help us grow all the flowers we gather and the vegetables we eat. The summer solstice is the day when the sun comes up the earliest and sets the latest, a long wonderful day in the summer and a time to celebrate. Bringing the garden to the table in many delectable forms, aromatic delights, and sensuous tastes. So why not have the table painted to celebrate the garden and the sun? Embrace the gifts of artists and artisans. Have your dishes handmade with chargers of chards from broken clay pots. The napkins, of course, must be hand-painted to reflect the pattern of the sun and patterns from the vegetable garden, the four quadrants—the four seasons. And to eat—appetizers include *tête do moin* cheese, olives, capers, berries, roasted red peppers, and elephant garlic. Braised Belgian endive, a zucchini and tomato gratin, and poached salmon with pesto were the main course and to follow fresh fig sorbet with fig alcohol—served in handmade footed fig leaves—what a delight. Although it is the season's longest day, the Summer Solstice is a day never long enough to fully appreciate all the riches and sustenance of the garden.

A sunflower sunburst detail from the table painted to celebrate the summer solstice dinner.

Above: The kitchen table became a composition of hors d'oeuvres, potted herbs that were massed as if growing together, and tomatoes in their own pot. *Kerria japonica* was picked from the garden and a wrought iron plant stand was used to arrange vegetables and fruit. *Opposite:* Chilled cantaloupe soup is served in my dining room. *Following pages:* Braised endive in a leaf dish cast from chards and a tomato gratin cooked and served in a piece of my own pottery embrace the idea of "handmade," giving a spirit of magical creativity when one embibes the garden through a culinary experience. Goat cheeses were presented in an antique Provençal cheese holder that would traditionally be mounted on a wall.

Above: Floral and foliage motifs appear on service pieces. This oak leaf pattern is a reproduction of an eighteenth-century design—yet another way the garden comes to the table. *Opposite:* Fig leaves were the inspiration for the fig sorbet created for the dessert. The artist even made fig feet for the leaves, which perpetuate the attention to detail that makes all the difference.

Reflection

The last flickering of the fireflies dot and dash in the darkened woods, and Pan sits silently waiting to play his flute. I am enticed to join him in celebrating the summer's end and take up my own flute, and with unconscious thought, words become notes that fill the quiet of the night with an unsung song of heart and soul. The fish, lying without motion on the bottom of the pool, do not shatter the stars captured on its surface. My own reflection in the moonlight tells me that this is not a dream.

I remember this past summer when it rained all season long and washed away the memories of drought from summers past. Certain plants thrived beyond expectations, others wilted and passed away and what was well intended never came to fruition. Looking back, what did thrive was a new experience and the continued assurance that we cannot have rain when we want it, nor sunshine, nor even the necessary cloudy day, but by living in accordance, each day will bring itself as a gift that will show us the way.

Leaves on trees above and around me are beginning to take on the hues of fall and, just as silently as the fireflies flicker, they begin to fall to the ground. All about the garden, subtle color schemes are being artfully emancipated, and planned combinations of forms and textures now take on a new light. Life itself begins to leave them behind. They, like me, have used the summer to collect thoughts that become enclosed in the trees' buds and seeds, branches and bark, becoming dormant and introspective, drained by the last days of summer's eve. They take on a new light as the garden becomes filled with colored leaves.

One day soon there will be enough leaves on the ground to rake them all into the driveway, but for now I let them fall where they may, for I love them on the ground as much as I do on the trees. What a moment of joy to lie in a bed of golden gingko leaves and rising up take full handfuls with me and throw them into the sky and watch them flutter back to the ground. I think I'll press a few and paste them on the wall of my sitting room. The ceiling is already papered with leaves, as a few years ago we collected leaves from a nearby umbrella magnolia. When you look up in that room in the winter, for a moment, fall is still there, as you sit and read. I now have my own umbrella magnolia, which has grown into a wonderful tree, and whenever there's patching to be done to the ceiling, I use my own leaves. Pressed ferns are embodied around the baseboard and some of the window panes have flower petals scattered about that bring colored light into the room when the sun comes inside on a winter's day, and thus the past—and the garden—remains with all my senses.

I remember becoming aware of trees because of my own great oak that for so long has provided cool shade for the visitors' garden. The ground beneath her bower is gently and dutifully raked in simple patterns on a daily basis, and the kitchen floor is swept and the tracked-in dirt thrown back into the yard. Raking takes me back to my childhood and our own dirt yard and the chinaberry trees that provided shade from the summer's heat—and the great branch to hang a swing on and fly as far as we could into the sky. Many hours were spent hiding from the rest of the world among her leaves, and wars were won between my brothers and me with spears made from her twigs. The berries themselves were collected and taken to school where we boiled and dyed them and then strung them into strings of multicolored pearls for our mother, who made sure we kept the yard tidy by raking up the fallen leaves. Then in the spring came great clusters of lavender flowers, and, though much time has passed, those flowers still smell the same to me as always. I now have my own chinaberry tree brought by a friend. Soon I'll have enough seed to make a necklace for myself.

We used to "play house" in the dirt of the yard and make mud pies. Then we would crawl underneath the house itself to while away some time coercing the doodle bugs to come out and play.

The autumnal equinox is nigh. Many changes are taking place in the garden. I made a list at the end of the day, and, upon rereading it, I realized that for once it wasn't filled with a lot of new ideas about having and getting but was more about relocating that which already exists. The moving of this to there, that to here, and some getting rid of and in whose place would go the one or two new things that were finally found and couldn't be lived without. Artfully and skillfully moving in and out without shattering the dream.

Her Memory Jar

"That is a pretty little Satsuma pot-pourri on your mantel." I said to a woman friend the other day.

"It is not a pot-pourri; it is a memory jar."

"A memory jar?" I repeated after her, forgetting my manners.

"Yes, it is a real clever idea, but it is not original with me. I got it from some paper or magazine. The jar is intended to hold souvenirs, especially flowers, though it is perfectly proper to drop in anything that is very precious. I have just begun mine. I ransacked my desk and bureau and made a start.

"This goldenrod is part of a bunch that 'he' picked for me one royal day last September when we were in the country. This faded maple leaf was picked up in Longfellow's yard. The pansies are some that Bella sent me commencement day; the fresher ones came from momma a few weeks ago. That unromantic looking twig came from a tree that Edgar A. Poe planted. I got it in Fordham one day when I made a pilgrimage there. The four-leaved clover was put in one of my favorite books by a friend who is dead. Everybody ought to keep a memory jar. Mine is becoming very interesting already."

And as she carefully put the cover on she said softly Jean Ingelow's words: "For memory is possession."

N.Y. Recorder
quoted in *The American Garden*
October, 1891

An idle moment under the scuppernong arbor with an antique basket of shirley poppies.

The essence of a day is captured by a quiet bath by candlelight, imbibing the "fruit of the vine" and the vespertine fragrance of an angel's trumpet.

ilhouettes and shadows create depth in a given space as well as evoke certain moods. One likes to spend summer afternoons beneath the cool shadow of a tree. That same tree, silhouetted against the winter sky, reveals its intricate inter-structure as if the life of the tree is mapped out against a blue sea. One can ponder the complexity of how such a grand tree can grow from such a small seed. It is with the shorter daylight hours that we become more cognizant of light and its effect in the garden. Light and shadow animate the garden and give its features presence. We can experience the spirit of the small angel bowing in reverence in a garden niche or feel the warmth that the sun brings by placing our hands on a garden wall. In this wall, a niche from an old church is enclosed and integrated into it, broken and disrupted by deciduous vines that seem to weave the feature together. The silhouette of a chair for the briefest of moments—emblazoned on an aged terra cotta pot. A bell in repose—when will the wind come and break the silence? Shall we take the time to sit or forever let it be a shadow that lurks in our mind? Only when the work is done can we reflect.

Bouquets

and arrangements are gathered thoughts, collected from the garden—perhaps on a walk to gather a nosegay for a friend. In August you might gather all the white flowers blooming in the garden, keeping in mind the nocturnal flowers—both in their flowering and the bouquet they might release only after the sun has passed. Add some golden foliage, some silver, and a few springs of variegated plants and contemplate designing a garden with those color schemes. Collect your blooms and foliage at all their different stages—not only as the blooms are just opening—as conventional wisdom would have it. Even the overblown bloom has character to give. Gather them (the rosebuds while ye may) in all seasons, for they are the gifts that are so easily shared—like a fresh bouquet garni for an evening meal.

Choose your plants with these ideas in mind so that even in the winter you can create your own *tableau vivant* depicting an eighteenth-century Flemish still life, combining fruits and vegetables with fresh flowers from the garden like camellias, wintersweet (*Chimonanthus praecox*), forget-me-nots, and the hellebores in bloom. Being the artist give it all a title. I called this one at right *Le jardin d'hiver*.

A bower woven of ivy, set atop the cake with a nosegay of roses, asters, Queen Anne's lace, and peegee hydrangea, nandina berries in their green form and from the garden in fall, tea blossoms from *Camellia sinensis*.

Above: Roses—Roses—Roses: 'Ballerina,' 'Nearly Wild,' 'Betty Prior,' 'Cécile Brünner,' and 'The Fairy' with Hollyhock, as a seedling, already doing her part, watching.

When the seasons change, each one subtly gives its grace and charm to the next—a transition that becomes a pleasant change of mood. Light changes, new flowers, old thoughts, new ideas, discovering what you had forgotten or where it was in your mind or in the garden. Picking a bouquet in fall of the last of the roses, *Rudbeckias,* and anemones, with a sprig of lemon balm to remind me of that wonderful tea cake I like to make—in a sea of golden ginkgo leaves—blending all the seasons together into one.

There are numerous ways to celebrate the joy that comes with making a garden and sharing those pleasures. For me, it's dogs, cats, and birds. Many of them have passed, yet they are still here as a part of the spirit of the place. Those that remain are equally as happy. Rosemary, Hollyhock, Snapper, and Joe-Pye Weed—captured here as a baby—he's still as innocent as he appears, and, no, he wasn't the one who crushed the peony buds. Willie's still here along with Cosmos—cats that run the place when the rest of us are at work. And Scooter and Jimmy Timmy (who left us for a better job) found out early it was more fun to hide in the tool box and dig holes in the ground.

Birds—with cats, no less—come in flocks as mixed as the flowers in the garden. I designed this bird feeder based on a late nineteenth-century building for storing potted plants for the winter, using small clay pots on a stacked stand for tasters' choice. I can easily see from my kitchen window forty-odd feet away. I can tell you, it's a successful addition to the garden—yet another way to share the bounty.

Autumn

comes more quietly than spring, but not without its own sense of values, colors, light. One soon starts to reflect; contentment eases in. Leaves swirl quietly to the ground laying a delicate pattern on the walk and grass. In the driveway there will soon be enough not to bother raking anymore. I sweep them all there so I can mow them and mulch the garden for the winter and help control weeds (the misplaced ones).

Yellows, oranges, browns, maroons, reds, greens—the rainbow has fallen from the sky and been absorbed by the leaves to disperse color throughout the garden. The bold texture of *Tetrapanax papyriferus* (rice paper plant) remains as a symbol of exotic, tropical lushness from the summer now gone. The *Miscanthus sinensis* 'Zebrinus,' or zebra grass, has set her plumy seed head to capture the last of the season's sun. It could be sad, I think, this passing, maybe a moment of nostalgia, as soothing as a digestif after a rich and splendid meal.

The *Hydrangea paniculata* 'Grandiflora,' trained as a standard, seems to be bowing in repose as summer passed by.

The golden-brown foliage of *Iris sibirica* denotes the change of season while this species of alstroemeria resurges with life as the weather cools.

Camellias got it hard in the frost of 1986, but I've planted many since then. If your weather won't allow for them, grow them in pots, for they bring such delight to a winter garden. *Camellia japonica* 'Debutante.'

Dinner on the Equinox

of autumn is held beneath a great white oak (*Quercus alba*). Folding screens inspired by tree trunks and *allées* divide the dirt driveway from the street as we sit to absorb the day and welcome the night of equal time.

Terra cotta chards were used to make table "follies" inspired by garden decorations. They were placed in a bed of sunflower seeds, baby corn, and peaches, which were also the ingredients used in the making of dinner. The grits casserole, molded in a nineteenth-century stoneware piece, was composed of garlic, heavy cream, corn-off-the-cob, and goat cheese. Seasoned with fresh herbs and onions from the garden, the chicken was baked with peach halves and prunes.

We were surrounded by a great sense of verdancy, and, as the twilight hour approached, the candles began to add a glowing nuance to the setting. The rustic fencing, the wrought iron chandelier and candelabra, and the use of burlap as a tablecloth brought a sense of earthiness to the dinner. Guatemalan candlesticks lighted the coffee table. Pottery cups from Mexico glazed with rich earthy tones of yellows, oranges, and browns seemed to envelop the evening. The titillating smell of fresh coffee rose in the air. Old-fashioned "hens and chicks" were clustered on a wire frame to create the incredible patterned topiary—again the garden brought to the table to celebrate its bounty. Served with port, a simple but classic flan made from MacIntosh apples ended the meal.

Indeed, the whole event seemed simple and pleasant—but when you eat out-of-doors among the trees and in the garden, should it not be that way?

Contentment

Contentment for the soul is not unlike a plant "going to seed." A time for rest and repose. I have remembered all my life the lines from Wordsworth's "The Daffodils": "for oft, when on my couch I lie / In vacant or in pensive mood . . ." Lines I take to heart each winter.

A part of each day is filled with getting ready to work in the garden. Like yesterday: a bit of tidying up, then into the garden to plant more hellebores (deep purple ones selected by a friend) in the visitors' garden and carefully choosing the site for the white buckeye that I had been waiting for for several years. Then taking a simple found stick and furrowing some rows in the vegetable garden for five types of lettuce. The peas were planted last week, as was the *Silybum*, which is now sprouting. A trade for a three-year-old *Crambe cordifolia* meant a serious walk in the borders to choose a spot with good sun and plenty of room, but with something to bloom later growing in front, as the crambe will bloom early and would leave a big void after it blooms its massive cloud form. Crambe creates one of those desired effects that one always seeks as it is experienced. I am content to try it now since I understand more of its needs to be successful in a Southern garden. In fact, I was contented with the whole day, but most of all with a few blank spots in the garden where I gently scratched the surface and blew poppy seed into the broken soil. It was like sowing joy.

Of course, the idea of contentment—like fulfillment, appreciation, and reflection—can occur in any season, but winter does bring each of us a time to rest and for the garden a time to sleep. For me it's an opportunity to read garden history, books about fragrance in the garden, and to pore over catalogues. I get all revved up about wanting this and that and should I try to grow the giant scotch thistle or not? Well, I didn't order many seed this year, only lettuces and nasturtiums. I was gratified by my own seed collection from the garden that filled my seed box. The little brown envelopes of cleomes, sunflowers, species zinnia, morning glories and moonvines, poppies, stone mountain daisies, and bidens is a treasure chest through which I often rummage, and I try to keep them in order of appropriate planting times. All throughout the seasons, there is an ongoing collection taking place, as different seed pods ripen. The dining room table soon becomes cluttered with bowls and plates filled with various pods. It's a feast unto itself, seed for thought. Years ago, my family always saved a certain amount of beans and corn for next year's vegetable garden and set back a few potatoes for "eyes" for next summer's crop.

There's always more seeds than I need, so I package carefully proportioned envelopes to send out in the mail—and hope that soon, in return, somebody will send me some *Cleome lutea* that I saw recently in a book. Wouldn't they be great bedded in the oval with all the other yellow and white annuals grown for the end of summer when that room in the garden is full of bloom?

They flash upon that inward eye
Which is the bliss of solitude;
And then my heart with pleasure fills,
And dances with the daffodils.
William Wordsworth

Billbergia nutans, commonly called "queen's tears," which I have grown, divided, and perpetuated for about twenty years, is one of the joys of the garden in winter, easily grown in a sunny window sill.

A Greenhouse

The greenhouses have been here since the '30s and '40s. The dugout came first and was built in 1919 and all are still in use. The dugout is used as a cold frame and for starting cool-weather crops from seed. The ivy house is aptly named and we create our own topiaries during the fall and winter months. Many are whimsical animal forms that become decorations for table settings or characters that "appear" in the garden.

Each November we receive our shipment of amaryllis and bring several hundred into successive bloom to celebrate Christmas at the shops. We mix them with paperwhites, maidenhair fern, ivies, and other cool-weather annuals to

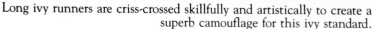
Long ivy runners are criss-crossed skillfully and artistically to create a superb camouflage for this ivy standard.

Christmas

create "flowering compositions" that perpetuate the old idea of dish gardens, once a staple of the flower industry. The Holcombe family created here their own mixed plantings for several decades—all from their own seed and cuttings—and for Mother's Day there were color-filled clay pots of geraniums, marigolds, dusty miller, petunias, and chrysanthemums—a garden in a pot. Maybe, one day when I take the time, I'll rejuvenate this idea with my own seedlings and cuttings.

A clipped privet makes a whimsical topiaried table for two to enjoy a chance warm winter's day. The antique flower basket is created from *Amaryllis* 'Wedding Dance' that were grown in the greenhouse.

The foliage house is filled with citrus, palms, clivia, ferns, scented geraniums, and other exotics that find their way into the garden in season. Last Christmas I thought why not have a cocktail party here as a prelude to our annual Christmas fete and as a celebration of contentment?

154

The greenhouse and the garden are the source for almost all the Christmas decorations. Amaryllis blossoms, loosely tucked among quilting lamps, and red-flowered passion vine ramble around a chest top. Lamp shades made from dried lotus leaves from the fish pond bring the garden inside to celebrate this special night. American holly (*Ilex opaca*), from a neighbor's yard, is a must when decorating for Christmas. I also grow lots of *Nandina domestica* and drape the chandelier with great clusters of its lovely red berries, and I weave asparagus fern (*Asparagus plumosus*) among all the lights.

I always have a little tree in a pot that is decorated from the garden with some "store-bought" chocolates from France. Dried sunflower heads from my *Helianthus annuus* are placed among the small boughs and are like the stars that fill the sky in the winter months. Garlands are made from the twining vines of *Cocculus carolinus* that were gathered from a barberry hedge found at a nearby train stop. After dinner, small candles are lighted for a moment of silence and the annual reading of e. e. cummings's poem written about the little tree who was sad to leave the forest but discovers the joy of being decorated and placed in a window where all could see her beauty and sing "Noel Noel."

The table in the dining room is draped with a cloth of silver-threaded silk saris that sparkle under candlelight. Votive cups—terra cotta tea infusers from China—provide soft twinkling among the place settings and the amaryllis, the red is called 'Bold Leader' and the white is 'Wedding Dance.' A stemmed service piece is laden with chartreuse seed pods gathered from the tendrils of the cruel vine that grows on the arbors. Wrought iron candelabra are swagged with more of the red-berried *C. carolinus* while a floor vase boasts *Leucothoe popifolia* and branches of nandina—all overflowing with the bounty of the garden.

A yule log is a tradition brought from the Old World that I embrace as a part of celebrating this season. Dusted with "powdered sugar snow" and garnished with wreath chocolates, holly sprigs, and hemlock twigs, the yule log is served on a mahogany tray my father brought back during WWII—all are precious memories to keep intact. A candelabra, simply adorned with more Carolina moon seed, creates a simple centerpiece for a table set with Provence plates with naïf interpretations of sunflowers and artichoke blossoms. The garden at every turn is brought to the table in a room whose ceiling is covered with the leaves of *Magnolia tripetala* that grows in the visitors' garden.

The Snow Is in My Hair

The snow is in my hair, the frost is in my frame,
The hopes of youth, in age can never be the same.

I would not have you suffer pain and vain regret,
Perhaps 'twere better that we both should now forget,

Though it has been a rare and wondrous episode
Upon life's wearisome and uneventful road.

But though, alas! our hands must tear themselves apart,
I still shall keep this lovely blossom of your heart,

The sweetest, dearest gift of life, to me, e'en though
To fullest bloom it may for neither of us grow.

With such delight I hold you in my heart's esteem
No minor chords can ever mar the happy dream.

'Tis only passion robs the casket of its gem,
But my pure thought stoops but to kiss your garment's hem;

The Primrose path my faithful feet have left untrod;
That door I have kept locked, and left the key with God;

It is to friendship all my votive lays belong,
And no regretful tears shall interrupt this song;

The memories of your ministry my life perfume,
And how can I forget you made the desert bloom?

—*James Terry White*

164

A snow cloud alights in the garden as the *Spiraea
Thunbergii* comes into blossom on warm winter days.

Snow

fell on the garden one night and I awoke to a silence one rarely experiences when you live in a city garden. But there it was outside every window, on every bough, like a great white blanket of the purest soft wool. Out into the garden I ran with all the dogs to see this magical moment in the early morning sun. Such a delight. All the arbors, gates, and paths were brought to a new life. The patterns on the ground, on the clipped hedges, seemed to emancipate the bones of the garden and I walked quietly through so as not to disturb this winter scene laid before me.

The silence was sublime,
and the peace and contentment that permeated my soul
made me know forever the pleasures of a garden well made and tended.
And in that moment
I became the well-placed weed.

Where will Spring be next Spring
in
our
hearts
cast about
like the flurry of petals on the
g
r
o
u
n
d
shall it be a passing thought
of all the glory that abounds
now that Spring is here.

Shall the summer bring us the same
delight
and flicker like the fireflies
in flight?

And when fall comes with her
leaves s
w
i
r
ling
d
o
w
n

with the frost of Winter
lying on the ground.

Where will we be—

Looking all around
out of the window

into the light.

Artistic and Horticultural Appreciation

Tom Woodham—a lifelong friend, for twenty years a business partner, for unending support of all my ideas.

Jeroy Hannah—who from the beginning—and even now—has brought his own form of creativity to the garden along with a compatible spirit.

Buck Newman, Jr.—his artistry permeates the house and captures the spirit of both home and garden in our theatrical experiences.

Smith Hanes III—whose love for vegetable gardening inspired me to make my own garden with his help.

Fred Brooks—who helped lay out the design for the borders and labored many hours with me to make this garden.

Marc Richardson and Richard Berry of Goodness Grows—who made it grow here.

Bud Heist of Heistaway Gardens—who grew so much from seed at my request and offered his own.

The Count Beauregard DuBois—whose extraordinary style captured the garden in many painterly settings on canvas and cutouts.

F.W. Thode—teacher and guide, who taught me that "when you walk through the garden, the garden must walk with you."

Denise Smith of GardenSmith—who grew so many of the vegetables from seed and is now growing my "dandelions."

Mike Norris and Company—who built the walls and paths with a love for stone equal to my love for flowers.

Mrs. Ruth Woodham—a friend, fellow gardener, and one who shared with me at the early age of learning to grow.

The Holcombe Family—who began the garden in the early part of this century and provided the legacy.

Rosemary Verey—who gave me the idea of embracing the history about gardening, without which we would not know where to begin.

Eve Davis—who gardens with the same fervor and love and shares both without end.

Chuck Domermuth—who fixes and builds with ingenuity and love.

Jimmy Rice—whose arbors scramble with roses and other vines.

Randy Alexander—without his devotion there would be no garden as it is now.

Brian Carter—who has helped me refine with an "added eye" (i).

Habersham Gardens—for their commitment to good horticulture.

Gary Coley—who brought the garden to the table as edible delights.

Christine Sibley—whose sculptural forms have created whimsy and amusement throughout the garden.

Grillo (Bob)—in the beginning, when there was nothing, we gathered from the ditches, roadsides, and railroad tracks.

Brooks Garcia—who artfully and skillfully rendered many of the plans and ideas onto paper and to fruition, including the plan of the garden for the endsheets.

Pat Chisholm—whose belief in me and unending support made me steadfast.

Mz. Fitch—whose *joie de vivre* enriches my garden.

Chad Stogner—whose mythological origins reproduce reality.

John Greenlee—whose gift of *Miscanthus* 'Morning Light' brings the sun into the garden.

Sharon Abroms—a fellow gardener whose knowledge includes the "joy" we all share that comes from weeding.

Sam Flowers—she brings the myths to fruition and embraces Dionysus.

All other friends, other gardens I have helped make, and my ever-changing staff who help me grow.

And last, but not least, the garden itself, without which I would have no soul.

Principal photography by David Schilling.
Other photography by:
Tom Woodham: pages 9, 14 top, 32, 44–45, 54 top, 56–57, 62–63, 64, 66, 68–69, 74–75, 78 bottom, 80 bottom, 122 bottom right, 138–139. *Brian Carter:* pages 98–99 bottom, 104–105 bottom 166–167 bottom, 167 top, 168–169. *Mick Hale:* pages 46–47, 59. *Bradley Newsom:* page 2. *Ryan Gainey:* pages 1, 14 bottom, 16 middle, 25, 29, 30 right, 31, 42 top, 48, 51, 52–53, 60 top, 72, 74 bottom, 76 top, 81 bottom, 98 top, 102 bottom, 114–115, 120–121, 122 bottom left, 126–129, 166 top, 170–173. The publisher is grateful to *Veranda* magazine for use of the following pictures: pages 84–93, 99, 101, 103, 106–113, 152.

"Her Memory Jar" was quoted in *The American Garden* in 1891.

"The Snow Is in My Hair," by James Terry White, was published in the book *A Garden of Remembrance* by Dodge Publishing Company, 1918.

Several of the garden pieces shown in this book have been reproduced as a part of the Ryan Gainey Collection. As a garden and floral designer I have a great reverence for the seasons and their gifts. As a Southerner I have a philosophical approach to life that embraces magic, charm, and romance. The items in this collection capture all of these nuances and will add a creative spirit and joy to everyday living. The pieces are available at The Potted Plant, 3165 East Shadowlawn Avenue, Atlanta, Georgia 30305 (404-233-7800) and The Cottage Garden, 2973 Hardman Court, Atlanta, Georgia 30305 (404-233-2050).

The Vegetable Garden

The Ivy House

The Barn

The
G

The Conservatory.

The
Pot
Terr

The Oval
Garden

The
Borders